CRYPTOCURRENCY
TRADING LOG BOOK

THIS BOOK BELONGS TO

NAME : _____

CONTACT : _____

ADDRESS : _____

CRYPTO
TRADING LOG BOOK

TRADING DETAILS

○ BUY ○ PROFIT	DATE TIME:	ENTRY PRICE:	PAIR:
○ SELL ○ LOSS	DATE TIME:	EXIT PRICE:	

MENTAL STATE   EXIT CONDITION

SETUP   NOTES

SATOSH W.L:_____ % OF ACCOUNT:_____ USD VALUE:_____

TRADING DETAILS

○ BUY ○ PROFIT	DATE TIME:	ENTRY PRICE:	PAIR:
○ SELL ○ LOSS	DATE TIME:	EXIT PRICE:	

MENTAL STATE   EXIT CONDITION

SETUP   NOTES

SATOSH W.L:_____ % OF ACCOUNT:_____ USD VALUE:_____

CRYPTO
TRADING LOG BOOK

TRADING DETAILS

| ○ BUY ○ PROFIT | DATE TIME: | ENTRY PRICE: | PAIR: |
| ○ SELL ○ LOSS | DATE TIME: | EXIT PRICE: | |

MENTRAL STATE | EXIT CONDITION

| |
| |
| |

| |
| |
| |

SETUP | NOTES

| |
| |
| |
| |

| |
| |
| |
| |

SATOSH W.L: _____ % OF ACCOUNT: _____ USD VALUE: _____

TRADING DETAILS

| ○ BUY ○ PROFIT | DATE TIME: | ENTRY PRICE: | PAIR: |
| ○ SELL ○ LOSS | DATE TIME: | EXIT PRICE: | |

MENTAL STATE | EXIT CONDITION

| |
| |
| |

| |
| |
| |

SETUP | NOTES

| |
| |
| |
| |

| |
| |
| |
| |

SATOSH W.L: _____ % OF ACCOUNT: _____ USD VALUE: _____

CRYPTO
TRADING LOG BOOK

TRADING DETAILS

○ BUY ○ PROFIT DATE TIME: ENTRY PRICE: PAIR:
○ SELL ○ LOSS   DATE TIME: EXIT PRICE:

MENTAL STATE   ## EXIT CONDITION

SETUP   ## NOTES

SATOSH W.L: _____ % OF ACCOUNT: _____ USD VALUE: _____

TRADING DETAILS

○ BUY ○ PROFIT DATE TIME: ENTRY PRICE: PAIR:
○ SELL ○ LOSS   DATE TIME: EXIT PRICE:

MENTAL STATE   ## EXIT CONDITION

SETUP   ## NOTES

SATOSH W.L: _____ % OF ACCOUNT: _____ USD VALUE: _____

CRYPTO
TRADING LOG BOOK

TRADING DETAILS

| ○ BUY   ○ PROFIT | DATE TIME: | ENTRY PRICE: | PAIR: |
| ○ SELL ○ LOSS | DATE TIME: | EXIT PRICE: | |

MENTAL STATE   ## EXIT CONDITION

SETUP   ## NOTES

SATOSH W.L:_____ % OF ACCOUNT:_____ USD VALUE:_____

TRADING DETAILS

| ○ BUY   ○ PROFIT | DATE TIME: | ENTRY PRICE: | PAIR: |
| ○ SELL ○ LOSS | DATE TIME: | EXIT PRICE: | |

MENTAL STATE   ## EXIT CONDITION

SETUP   ## NOTES

SATOSH W.L:_____ % OF ACCOUNT:_____ USD VALUE:_____

CRYPTO
TRADING LOG BOOK

TRADING DETAILS

○ BUY ○ PROFIT DATE TIME: ENTRY PRICE: PAIR:
○ SELL ○ LOSS DATE TIME: EXIT PRICE:

MENTAL STATE

EXIT CONDITION

SETUP

NOTES

SATOSH W.L: _____ % OF ACCOUNT: _____ USD VALUE: _____

TRADING DETAILS

○ BUY ○ PROFIT DATE TIME: ENTRY PRICE: PAIR:
○ SELL ○ LOSS DATE TIME: EXIT PRICE:

MENTAL STATE

EXIT CONDITION

SETUP

NOTES

SATOSH W.L: _____ % OF ACCOUNT: _____ USD VALUE: _____

CRYPTO
TRADING LOG BOOK

TRADING DETAILS

○ BUY ○ PROFIT	DATE TIME:	ENTRY PRICE:	PAIR:
○ SELL ○ LOSS	DATE TIME:	EXIT PRICE:	

MENTAL STATE

EXIT CONDITION

SETUP

NOTES

SATOSH W.L: _____ % OF ACCOUNT: _____ USD VALUE: _____

TRADING DETAILS

○ BUY ○ PROFIT	DATE TIME:	ENTRY PRICE:	PAIR:
○ SELL ○ LOSS	DATE TIME:	EXIT PRICE:	

MENTAL STATE

EXIT CONDITION

SETUP

NOTES

SATOSH W.L: _____ % OF ACCOUNT: _____ USD VALUE: _____

CRYPTO
TRADING LOG BOOK

TRADING DETAILS

| ○ BUY   ○ PROFIT | DATE TIME: | ENTRY PRICE: | PAIR: |
| ○ SELL ○ LOSS | DATE TIME: | EXIT PRICE: | |

MENTAL STATE

EXIT CONDITION

SETUP

NOTES

SATOSH W.L:_____ % OF ACCOUNT:_____ USD VALUE:_____

TRADING DETAILS

| ○ BUY   ○ PROFIT | DATE TIME: | ENTRY PRICE: | PAIR: |
| ○ SELL ○ LOSS | DATE TIME: | EXIT PRICE: | |

MENTAL STATE

EXIT CONDITION

SETUP

NOTES

SATOSH W.L:_____ % OF ACCOUNT:_____ USD VALUE:_____

CRYPTO
TRADING LOG BOOK

TRADING DETAILS

○ BUY ○ PROFIT	DATE TIME:	ENTRY PRICE:	PAIR:
○ SELL ○ LOSS	DATE TIME:	EXIT PRICE:	

MENTAL STATE

EXIT CONDITION

SETUP

NOTES

SATOSH W.L: _____ % OF ACCOUNT: _____ USD VALUE: _____

TRADING DETAILS

○ BUY ○ PROFIT	DATE TIME:	ENTRY PRICE:	PAIR:
○ SELL ○ LOSS	DATE TIME:	EXIT PRICE:	

MENTAL STATE

EXIT CONDITION

SETUP

NOTES

SATOSH W.L: _____ % OF ACCOUNT: _____ USD VALUE: _____

CRYPTO
TRADING LOG BOOK

TRADING DETAILS

○ BUY   ○ PROFIT   DATE TIME: _____   ENTRY PRICE: _____   PAIR: _____
○ SELL ○ LOSS   DATE TIME: _____   EXIT PRICE: _____

MENTAL STATE

EXIT CONDITION

SETUP

NOTES

SATOSH W.L: _____   % OF ACCOUNT: _____   USD VALUE: _____

TRADING DETAILS

○ BUY   ○ PROFIT   DATE TIME: _____   ENTRY PRICE: _____   PAIR: _____
○ SELL ○ LOSS   DATE TIME: _____   EXIT PRICE: _____

MENTAL STATE

EXIT CONDITION

SETUP

NOTES

SATOSH W.L: _____   % OF ACCOUNT: _____   USD VALUE: _____

CRYPTO
TRADING LOG BOOK

TRADING DETAILS

◯ BUY ◯ PROFIT	DATE TIME:	ENTRY PRICE:	PAIR:
◯ SELL ◯ LOSS	DATE TIME:	EXIT PRICE:	

MENTRAL STATE

EXIT CONDITION

SETUP

NOTES

SATOSH W.L: _____ % OF ACCOUNT: _____ USD VALUE: _____

TRADING DETAILS

◯ BUY ◯ PROFIT	DATE TIME:	ENTRY PRICE:	PAIR:
◯ SELL ◯ LOSS	DATE TIME:	EXIT PRICE:	

MENTAL STATE

EXIT CONDITION

SETUP

NOTES

SATOSH W.L: _____ % OF ACCOUNT: _____ USD VALUE: _____

CRYPTO
TRADING LOG BOOK

TRADING DETAILS

○ BUY ○ PROFIT	DATE TIME:	ENTRY PRICE:	PAIR:
○ SELL ○ LOSS	DATE TIME:	EXIT PRICE:	

MENTAL STATE

EXIT CONDITION

SETUP

NOTES

SATOSH W.L:_____ % OF ACCOUNT: _____ USD VALUE: _____

TRADING DETAILS

○ BUY ○ PROFIT	DATE TIME:	ENTRY PRICE:	PAIR:
○ SELL ○ LOSS	DATE TIME:	EXIT PRICE:	

MENTAL STATE

EXIT CONDITION

SETUP

NOTES

SATOSH W.L:_____ % OF ACCOUNT: _____ USD VALUE: _____

CRYPTO
TRADING LOG BOOK

TRADING DETAILS

○ BUY ○ PROFIT	DATE TIME:	ENTRY PRICE:	PAIR:
○ SELL ○ LOSS	DATE TIME:	EXIT PRICE:	

MENTAL STATE

EXIT CONDITION

SETUP

NOTES

SATOSH W.L: _____ % OF ACCOUNT: _____ USD VALUE: _____

TRADING DETAILS

○ BUY ○ PROFIT	DATE TIME:	ENTRY PRICE:	PAIR:
○ SELL ○ LOSS	DATE TIME:	EXIT PRICE:	

MENTAL STATE

EXIT CONDITION

SETUP

NOTES

SATOSH W.L: _____ % OF ACCOUNT: _____ USD VALUE: _____

CRYPTO
TRADING LOG BOOK

TRADING DETAILS

○ BUY ○ PROFIT	DATE TIME:	ENTRY PRICE:	PAIR:
○ SELL ○ LOSS	DATE TIME:	EXIT PRICE:	

MENTAL STATE

EXIT CONDITION

SETUP

NOTES

SATOSH W.L: _____ % OF ACCOUNT: _____ USD VALUE: _____

TRADING DETAILS

○ BUY ○ PROFIT	DATE TIME:	ENTRY PRICE:	PAIR:
○ SELL ○ LOSS	DATE TIME:	EXIT PRICE:	

MENTAL STATE

EXIT CONDITION

SETUP

NOTES

SATOSH W.L: _____ % OF ACCOUNT: _____ USD VALUE: _____

CRYPTO
TRADING LOG BOOK

TRADING DETAILS

| ○ BUY ○ PROFIT | DATE TIME: | ENTRY PRICE: | PAIR: |
| ○ SELL ○ LOSS | DATE TIME: | EXIT PRICE: | |

MENTAL STATE

EXIT CONDITION

SETUP

NOTES

SATOSH W.L: _____ % OF ACCOUNT: _____ USD VALUE: _____

TRADING DETAILS

| ○ BUY ○ PROFIT | DATE TIME: | ENTRY PRICE: | PAIR: |
| ○ SELL ○ LOSS | DATE TIME: | EXIT PRICE: | |

MENTAL STATE

EXIT CONDITION

SETUP

NOTES

SATOSH W.L: _____ % OF ACCOUNT: _____ USD VALUE: _____

CRYPTO
TRADING LOG BOOK

TRADING DETAILS

| ○ BUY ○ PROFIT | DATE TIME: | ENTRY PRICE: | PAIR: |
| ○ SELL ○ LOSS | DATE TIME: | EXIT PRICE: | |

MENTAL STATE

EXIT CONDITION

SETUP

NOTES

SATOSH W.L: _____ % OF ACCOUNT: _____ USD VALUE: _____

TRADING DETAILS

| ○ BUY ○ PROFIT | DATE TIME: | ENTRY PRICE: | PAIR: |
| ○ SELL ○ LOSS | DATE TIME: | EXIT PRICE: | |

MENTAL STATE

EXIT CONDITION

SETUP

NOTES

SATOSH W.L: _____ % OF ACCOUNT: _____ USD VALUE: _____

CRYPTO
TRADING LOG BOOK

TRADING DETAILS

○ BUY ○ PROFIT   DATE TIME: ENTRY PRICE: PAIR:
○ SELL ○ LOSS   DATE TIME: EXIT PRICE:

MENTAL STATE   ## EXIT CONDITION

SETUP   ## NOTES

SATOSH W.L: _____ % OF ACCOUNT: _____ USD VALUE: _____

TRADING DETAILS

○ BUY ○ PROFIT   DATE TIME: ENTRY PRICE: PAIR:
○ SELL ○ LOSS   DATE TIME: EXIT PRICE:

MENTAL STATE   ## EXIT CONDITION

SETUP   ## NOTES

SATOSH W.L: _____ % OF ACCOUNT: _____ USD VALUE: _____

CRYPTO
TRADING LOG BOOK

TRADING DETAILS

○ BUY ○ PROFIT	DATE TIME:	ENTRY PRICE:	PAIR:
○ SELL ○ LOSS	DATE TIME:	EXIT PRICE:	

MENTAL STATE
EXIT CONDITION

SETUP
NOTES

SATOSH W.L:_____ % OF ACCOUNT:_____ USD VALUE:_____

TRADING DETAILS

○ BUY ○ PROFIT	DATE TIME:	ENTRY PRICE:	PAIR:
○ SELL ○ LOSS	DATE TIME:	EXIT PRICE:	

MENTAL STATE
EXIT CONDITION

SETUP
NOTES

SATOSH W.L:_____ % OF ACCOUNT:_____ USD VALUE:_____

CRYPTO
TRADING LOG BOOK

TRADING DETAILS

| ○ BUY ○ PROFIT | DATE TIME: | ENTRY PRICE: | PAIR: |
| ○ SELL ○ LOSS | DATE TIME: | EXIT PRICE: | |

MENTRAL STATE

EXIT CONDITION

SETUP

NOTES

SATOSH W.L:_____ % OF ACCOUNT:_____ USD VALUE:_____

TRADING DETAILS

| ○ BUY ○ PROFIT | DATE TIME: | ENTRY PRICE: | PAIR: |
| ○ SELL ○ LOSS | DATE TIME: | EXIT PRICE: | |

MENTAL STATE

EXIT CONDITION

SETUP

NOTES

SATOSH W.L:_____ % OF ACCOUNT:_____ USD VALUE:_____

CRYPTO
TRADING LOG BOOK

TRADING DETAILS

| ○ BUY   ○ PROFIT | DATE TIME: | ENTRY PRICE: | PAIR: |
| ○ SELL ○ LOSS | DATE TIME: | EXIT PRICE: | |

MENTRAL STATE

EXIT CONDITION

SETUP

NOTES

SATOSH W.L: _____ % OF ACCOUNT: _____ USD VALUE: _____

TRADING DETAILS

| ○ BUY   ○ PROFIT | DATE TIME: | ENTRY PRICE: | PAIR: |
| ○ SELL ○ LOSS | DATE TIME: | EXIT PRICE: | |

MENTAL STATE

EXIT CONDITION

SETUP

NOTES

SATOSH W.L: _____ % OF ACCOUNT: _____ USD VALUE: _____

CRYPTO
TRADING LOG BOOK

TRADING DETAILS

○ BUY ○ PROFIT	DATE TIME:	ENTRY PRICE:	PAIR:
○ SELL ○ LOSS	DATE TIME:	EXIT PRICE:	

MENTAL STATE

EXIT CONDITION

SETUP

NOTES

SATOSH W.L: _____ % OF ACCOUNT: _____ USD VALUE: _____

TRADING DETAILS

○ BUY ○ PROFIT	DATE TIME:	ENTRY PRICE:	PAIR:
○ SELL ○ LOSS	DATE TIME:	EXIT PRICE:	

MENTAL STATE

EXIT CONDITION

SETUP

NOTES

SATOSH W.L: _____ % OF ACCOUNT: _____ USD VALUE: _____

CRYPTO
TRADING LOG BOOK

TRADING DETAILS

| ○ BUY   ○ PROFIT | DATE TIME: | ENTRY PRICE: | PAIR: |
| ○ SELL ○ LOSS | DATE TIME: | EXIT PRICE: | |

MENTAL STATE

EXIT CONDITION

SETUP

NOTES

SATOSH W.L: _____ % OF ACCOUNT: _____ USD VALUE: _____

TRADING DETAILS

| ○ BUY   ○ PROFIT | DATE TIME: | ENTRY PRICE: | PAIR: |
| ○ SELL ○ LOSS | DATE TIME: | EXIT PRICE: | |

MENTAL STATE

EXIT CONDITION

SETUP

NOTES

SATOSH W.L: _____ % OF ACCOUNT: _____ USD VALUE: _____

CRYPTO
TRADING LOG BOOK

TRADING DETAILS

| ○ BUY   ○ PROFIT | DATE TIME: | ENTRY PRICE: | PAIR: |
| ○ SELL ○ LOSS | DATE TIME: | EXIT PRICE: | |

MENTRAL STATE

EXIT CONDITION

SETUP

NOTES

SATOSH W.L: _____ % OF ACCOUNT: _____ USD VALUE: _____

TRADING DETAILS

| ○ BUY   ○ PROFIT | DATE TIME: | ENTRY PRICE: | PAIR: |
| ○ SELL ○ LOSS | DATE TIME: | EXIT PRICE: | |

MENTAL STATE

EXIT CONDITION

SETUP

NOTES

SATOSH W.L: _____ % OF ACCOUNT: _____ USD VALUE: _____

CRYPTO

TRADING LOG BOOK

TRADING DETAILS

| ○ BUY   ○ PROFIT | DATE TIME: | ENTRY PRICE: | PAIR: |
| ○ SELL ○ LOSS | DATE TIME: | EXIT PRICE: | |

MENTAL STATE

EXIT CONDITION

SETUP

NOTES

SATOSH W.L:_____ % OF ACCOUNT: _____ USD VALUE: _____

TRADING DETAILS

| ○ BUY   ○ PROFIT | DATE TIME: | ENTRY PRICE: | PAIR: |
| ○ SELL ○ LOSS | DATE TIME: | EXIT PRICE: | |

MENTAL STATE

EXIT CONDITION

SETUP

NOTES

SATOSH W.L:_____ % OF ACCOUNT: _____ USD VALUE: _____

CRYPTO
TRADING LOG BOOK

TRADING DETAILS

○ BUY ○ PROFIT	DATE TIME:	ENTRY PRICE:	PAIR:
○ SELL ○ LOSS	DATE TIME:	EXIT PRICE:	

MENTAL STATE

EXIT CONDITION

SETUP

NOTES

SATOSH W.L: _____ % OF ACCOUNT: _____ USD VALUE: _____

TRADING DETAILS

○ BUY ○ PROFIT	DATE TIME:	ENTRY PRICE:	PAIR:
○ SELL ○ LOSS	DATE TIME:	EXIT PRICE:	

MENTAL STATE

EXIT CONDITION

SETUP

NOTES

SATOSH W.L: _____ % OF ACCOUNT: _____ USD VALUE: _____

CRYPTO
TRADING LOG BOOK

TRADING DETAILS

- ○ BUY ○ PROFIT DATE TIME: ENTRY PRICE: PAIR:
- ○ SELL ○ LOSS   DATE TIME: EXIT PRICE:

MENTAL STATE

EXIT CONDITION

SETUP

NOTES

SATOSH W.L: _____ % OF ACCOUNT: _____ USD VALUE: _____

TRADING DETAILS

- ○ BUY ○ PROFIT DATE TIME: ENTRY PRICE: PAIR:
- ○ SELL ○ LOSS   DATE TIME: EXIT PRICE:

MENTAL STATE

EXIT CONDITION

SETUP

NOTES

SATOSH W.L: _____ % OF ACCOUNT: _____ USD VALUE: _____

CRYPTO
TRADING LOG BOOK

TRADING DETAILS

| ○ BUY   ○ PROFIT | DATE TIME: | ENTRY PRICE: | PAIR: |
| ○ SELL ○ LOSS | DATE TIME: | EXIT PRICE: | |

MENTRAL STATE   EXIT CONDITION

SETUP   NOTES

SATOSH W.L: _____ % OF ACCOUNT: _____ USD VALUE: _____

TRADING DETAILS

| ○ BUY   ○ PROFIT | DATE TIME: | ENTRY PRICE: | PAIR: |
| ○ SELL ○ LOSS | DATE TIME: | EXIT PRICE: | |

MENTAL STATE   EXIT CONDITION

SETUP   NOTES

SATOSH W.L: _____ % OF ACCOUNT: _____ USD VALUE: _____

CRYPTO
TRADING LOG BOOK

TRADING DETAILS

| ○ BUY ○ PROFIT | DATE TIME: | ENTRY PRICE: | PAIR: |
| ○ SELL ○ LOSS | DATE TIME: | EXIT PRICE: | |

MENTAL STATE

EXIT CONDITION

SETUP

NOTES

SATOSH W.L:_____ % OF ACCOUNT:_____ USD VALUE:_____

TRADING DETAILS

| ○ BUY ○ PROFIT | DATE TIME: | ENTRY PRICE: | PAIR: |
| ○ SELL ○ LOSS | DATE TIME: | EXIT PRICE: | |

MENTAL STATE

EXIT CONDITION

SETUP

NOTES

SATOSH W.L:_____ % OF ACCOUNT:_____ USD VALUE:_____

CRYPTO
TRADING LOG BOOK

TRADING DETAILS

○ BUY ○ PROFIT	DATE TIME:	ENTRY PRICE:	PAIR:
○ SELL ○ LOSS	DATE TIME:	EXIT PRICE:	

MENTAL STATE

EXIT CONDITION

SETUP

NOTES

SATOSH W.L: _____ % OF ACCOUNT: _____ USD VALUE: _____

TRADING DETAILS

○ BUY ○ PROFIT	DATE TIME:	ENTRY PRICE:	PAIR:
○ SELL ○ LOSS	DATE TIME:	EXIT PRICE:	

MENTAL STATE

EXIT CONDITION

SETUP

NOTES

SATOSH W.L: _____ % OF ACCOUNT: _____ USD VALUE: _____

CRYPTO
TRADING LOG BOOK

TRADING DETAILS

| ○ BUY ○ PROFIT | DATE TIME: | ENTRY PRICE: | PAIR: |
| ○ SELL ○ LOSS | DATE TIME: | EXIT PRICE: | |

MENTAL STATE

EXIT CONDITION

SETUP

NOTES

SATOSH W.L: _____ % OF ACCOUNT: _____ USD VALUE: _____

TRADING DETAILS

| ○ BUY ○ PROFIT | DATE TIME: | ENTRY PRICE: | PAIR: |
| ○ SELL ○ LOSS | DATE TIME: | EXIT PRICE: | |

MENTAL STATE

EXIT CONDITION

SETUP

NOTES

SATOSH W.L: _____ % OF ACCOUNT: _____ USD VALUE: _____

CRYPTO
TRADING LOG BOOK

TRADING DETAILS

○ BUY   ○ PROFIT   DATE TIME: ENTRY PRICE: PAIR:
○ SELL ○ LOSS   DATE TIME: EXIT PRICE:

MENTAL STATE

EXIT CONDITION

SETUP

NOTES

SATOSH W.L: _____ % OF ACCOUNT: _____ USD VALUE: _____

TRADING DETAILS

○ BUY   ○ PROFIT   DATE TIME: ENTRY PRICE: PAIR:
○ SELL ○ LOSS   DATE TIME: EXIT PRICE:

MENTAL STATE

EXIT CONDITION

SETUP

NOTES

SATOSH W.L: _____ % OF ACCOUNT: _____ USD VALUE: _____

CRYPTO
TRADING LOG BOOK

TRADING DETAILS

○ BUY ○ PROFIT	DATE TIME:	ENTRY PRICE:	PAIR:
○ SELL ○ LOSS	DATE TIME:	EXIT PRICE:	

MENTAL STATE

EXIT CONDITION

SETUP

NOTES

SATOSH W.L:_____ % OF ACCOUNT:_____ USD VALUE:_____

TRADING DETAILS

○ BUY ○ PROFIT	DATE TIME:	ENTRY PRICE:	PAIR:
○ SELL ○ LOSS	DATE TIME:	EXIT PRICE:	

MENTAL STATE

EXIT CONDITION

SETUP

NOTES

SATOSH W.L:_____ % OF ACCOUNT:_____ USD VALUE:_____

CRYPTO
TRADING LOG BOOK

TRADING DETAILS

- ◯ BUY ◯ PROFIT
- ◯ SELL ◯ LOSS

DATE TIME:
DATE TIME:

ENTRY PRICE:
EXIT PRICE:

PAIR:

MENTAL STATE

EXIT CONDITION

SETUP

NOTES

SATOSH W.L: _____ % OF ACCOUNT: _____ USD VALUE: _____

TRADING DETAILS

- ◯ BUY ◯ PROFIT
- ◯ SELL ◯ LOSS

DATE TIME:
DATE TIME:

ENTRY PRICE:
EXIT PRICE:

PAIR:

MENTAL STATE

EXIT CONDITION

SETUP

NOTES

SATOSH W.L: _____ % OF ACCOUNT: _____ USD VALUE: _____

CRYPTO
TRADING LOG BOOK

TRADING DETAILS

| ○ BUY   ○ PROFIT | DATE TIME: | ENTRY PRICE: | PAIR: |
| ○ SELL ○ LOSS | DATE TIME: | EXIT PRICE: | |

MENTAL STATE

EXIT CONDITION

SETUP

NOTES

SATOSH W.L:_____ % OF ACCOUNT:_____ USD VALUE:_____

TRADING DETAILS

| ○ BUY   ○ PROFIT | DATE TIME: | ENTRY PRICE: | PAIR: |
| ○ SELL ○ LOSS | DATE TIME: | EXIT PRICE: | |

MENTAL STATE

EXIT CONDITION

SETUP

NOTES

SATOSH W.L:_____ % OF ACCOUNT:_____ USD VALUE:_____

CRYPTO
TRADING LOG BOOK

TRADING DETAILS

○ BUY ○ PROFIT	DATE TIME:	ENTRY PRICE:	PAIR:
○ SELL ○ LOSS	DATE TIME:	EXIT PRICE:	

MENTAL STATE

EXIT CONDITION

SETUP

NOTES

SATOSH W.L: _____ % OF ACCOUNT: _____ USD VALUE: _____

TRADING DETAILS

○ BUY ○ PROFIT	DATE TIME:	ENTRY PRICE:	PAIR:
○ SELL ○ LOSS	DATE TIME:	EXIT PRICE:	

MENTAL STATE

EXIT CONDITION

SETUP

NOTES

SATOSH W.L: _____ % OF ACCOUNT: _____ USD VALUE: _____

CRYPTO
TRADING LOG BOOK

TRADING DETAILS

| ○ BUY ○ PROFIT | DATE TIME: | ENTRY PRICE: | PAIR: |
| ○ SELL ○ LOSS | DATE TIME: | EXIT PRICE: | |

MENTRAL STATE

EXIT CONDITION

SETUP

NOTES

SATOSH W.L: _____ % OF ACCOUNT: _____ USD VALUE: _____

TRADING DETAILS

| ○ BUY ○ PROFIT | DATE TIME: | ENTRY PRICE: | PAIR: |
| ○ SELL ○ LOSS | DATE TIME: | EXIT PRICE: | |

MENTAL STATE

EXIT CONDITION

SETUP

NOTES

SATOSH W.L: _____ % OF ACCOUNT: _____ USD VALUE: _____

CRYPTO
TRADING LOG BOOK

TRADING DETAILS

○ BUY ○ PROFIT	DATE TIME:	ENTRY PRICE:	PAIR:
○ SELL ○ LOSS	DATE TIME:	EXIT PRICE:	

MENTAL STATE

EXIT CONDITION

SETUP

NOTES

SATOSH W.L: _____ % OF ACCOUNT: _____ USD VALUE: _____

TRADING DETAILS

○ BUY ○ PROFIT	DATE TIME:	ENTRY PRICE:	PAIR:
○ SELL ○ LOSS	DATE TIME:	EXIT PRICE:	

MENTAL STATE

EXIT CONDITION

SETUP

NOTES

SATOSH W.L: _____ % OF ACCOUNT: _____ USD VALUE: _____

CRYPTO
TRADING LOG BOOK

TRADING DETAILS

| ○ BUY ○ PROFIT | DATE TIME: | ENTRY PRICE: | PAIR: |
| ○ SELL ○ LOSS | DATE TIME: | EXIT PRICE: | |

MENTAL STATE

EXIT CONDITION

SETUP

NOTES

SATOSH W.L:_____ % OF ACCOUNT:_____ USD VALUE:_____

TRADING DETAILS

| ○ BUY ○ PROFIT | DATE TIME: | ENTRY PRICE: | PAIR: |
| ○ SELL ○ LOSS | DATE TIME: | EXIT PRICE: | |

MENTAL STATE

EXIT CONDITION

SETUP

NOTES

SATOSH W.L:_____ % OF ACCOUNT:_____ USD VALUE:_____

CRYPTO
TRADING LOG BOOK

TRADING DETAILS

| ○ BUY   ○ PROFIT | DATE TIME: | ENTRY PRICE: | PAIR: |
| ○ SELL   ○ LOSS | DATE TIME: | EXIT PRICE: | |

MENTAL STATE

EXIT CONDITION

SETUP

NOTES

SATOSH W.L: _____ % OF ACCOUNT: _____ USD VALUE: _____

TRADING DETAILS

| ○ BUY   ○ PROFIT | DATE TIME: | ENTRY PRICE: | PAIR: |
| ○ SELL   ○ LOSS | DATE TIME: | EXIT PRICE: | |

MENTAL STATE

EXIT CONDITION

SETUP

NOTES

SATOSH W.L: _____ % OF ACCOUNT: _____ USD VALUE: _____

CRYPTO
TRADING LOG BOOK

TRADING DETAILS

| ○ BUY   ○ PROFIT | DATE TIME: | ENTRY PRICE: | PAIR: |
| ○ SELL ○ LOSS | DATE TIME: | EXIT PRICE: | |

MENTAL STATE

EXIT CONDITION

SETUP

NOTES

SATOSH W.L:_____ % OF ACCOUNT:_____ USD VALUE:_____

TRADING DETAILS

| ○ BUY   ○ PROFIT | DATE TIME: | ENTRY PRICE: | PAIR: |
| ○ SELL ○ LOSS | DATE TIME: | EXIT PRICE: | |

MENTAL STATE

EXIT CONDITION

SETUP

NOTES

SATOSH W.L:_____ % OF ACCOUNT:_____ USD VALUE:_____

CRYPTO
TRADING LOG BOOK

TRADING DETAILS

○ BUY ○ PROFIT	DATE TIME:	ENTRY PRICE:	PAIR:
○ SELL ○ LOSS	DATE TIME:	EXIT PRICE:	

MENTAL STATE

EXIT CONDITION

SETUP

NOTES

SATOSH W.L:_____ % OF ACCOUNT:_____ USD VALUE:_____

TRADING DETAILS

○ BUY ○ PROFIT	DATE TIME:	ENTRY PRICE:	PAIR:
○ SELL ○ LOSS	DATE TIME:	EXIT PRICE:	

MENTAL STATE

EXIT CONDITION

SETUP

NOTES

SATOSH W.L:_____ % OF ACCOUNT:_____ USD VALUE:_____

CRYPTO
TRADING LOG BOOK

TRADING DETAILS

| ○ BUY ○ PROFIT | DATE TIME: | ENTRY PRICE: | PAIR: |
| ○ SELL ○ LOSS | DATE TIME: | EXIT PRICE: | |

MENTAL STATE

EXIT CONDITION

SETUP

NOTES

SATOSH W.L: _____ % OF ACCOUNT: _____ USD VALUE: _____

TRADING DETAILS

| ○ BUY ○ PROFIT | DATE TIME: | ENTRY PRICE: | PAIR: |
| ○ SELL ○ LOSS | DATE TIME: | EXIT PRICE: | |

MENTAL STATE

EXIT CONDITION

SETUP

NOTES

SATOSH W.L: _____ % OF ACCOUNT: _____ USD VALUE: _____

CRYPTO
TRADING LOG BOOK

TRADING DETAILS

| ○ BUY   ○ PROFIT | DATE TIME: | ENTRY PRICE: | PAIR: |
| ○ SELL ○ LOSS | DATE TIME: | EXIT PRICE: | |

MENTRAL STATE

EXIT CONDITION

SETUP

NOTES

SATOSH W.L: _____ % OF ACCOUNT: _____ USD VALUE: _____

TRADING DETAILS

| ○ BUY   ○ PROFIT | DATE TIME: | ENTRY PRICE: | PAIR: |
| ○ SELL ○ LOSS | DATE TIME: | EXIT PRICE: | |

MENTAL STATE

EXIT CONDITION

SETUP

NOTES

SATOSH W.L: _____ % OF ACCOUNT: _____ USD VALUE: _____

CRYPTO
TRADING LOG BOOK

TRADING DETAILS

○ BUY ○ PROFIT	DATE TIME:	ENTRY PRICE:	PAIR:
○ SELL ○ LOSS	DATE TIME:	EXIT PRICE:	

MENTAL STATE

EXIT CONDITION

SETUP

NOTES

SATOSH W.L:_____ % OF ACCOUNT:_____ USD VALUE:_____

TRADING DETAILS

○ BUY ○ PROFIT	DATE TIME:	ENTRY PRICE:	PAIR:
○ SELL ○ LOSS	DATE TIME:	EXIT PRICE:	

MENTAL STATE

EXIT CONDITION

SETUP

NOTES

SATOSH W.L:_____ % OF ACCOUNT:_____ USD VALUE:_____

CRYPTO
TRADING LOG BOOK

TRADING DETAILS

| ○ BUY ○ PROFIT | DATE TIME: | ENTRY PRICE: | PAIR: |
| ○ SELL ○ LOSS | DATE TIME: | EXIT PRICE: | |

MENTAL STATE

EXIT CONDITION

SETUP

NOTES

SATOSH W.L:_____ % OF ACCOUNT:_____ USD VALUE:_____

TRADING DETAILS

| ○ BUY ○ PROFIT | DATE TIME: | ENTRY PRICE: | PAIR: |
| ○ SELL ○ LOSS | DATE TIME: | EXIT PRICE: | |

MENTAL STATE

EXIT CONDITION

SETUP

NOTES

SATOSH W.L:_____ % OF ACCOUNT:_____ USD VALUE:_____

CRYPTO
TRADING LOG BOOK

TRADING DETAILS

| ○ BUY ○ PROFIT | DATE TIME: | ENTRY PRICE: | PAIR: |
| ○ SELL ○ LOSS | DATE TIME: | EXIT PRICE: | |

MENTAL STATE

EXIT CONDITION

SETUP

NOTES

SATOSH W.L: _____ % OF ACCOUNT: _____ USD VALUE: _____

TRADING DETAILS

| ○ BUY ○ PROFIT | DATE TIME: | ENTRY PRICE: | PAIR: |
| ○ SELL ○ LOSS | DATE TIME: | EXIT PRICE: | |

MENTAL STATE

EXIT CONDITION

SETUP

NOTES

SATOSH W.L: _____ % OF ACCOUNT: _____ USD VALUE: _____

CRYPTO
TRADING LOG BOOK

TRADING DETAILS

○ BUY ○ PROFIT	DATE TIME:	ENTRY PRICE:	PAIR:
○ SELL ○ LOSS	DATE TIME:	EXIT PRICE:	

MENTAL STATE

EXIT CONDITION

SETUP

NOTES

SATOSH W.L: _____ % OF ACCOUNT: _____ USD VALUE: _____

TRADING DETAILS

○ BUY ○ PROFIT	DATE TIME:	ENTRY PRICE:	PAIR:
○ SELL ○ LOSS	DATE TIME:	EXIT PRICE:	

MENTAL STATE

EXIT CONDITION

SETUP

NOTES

SATOSH W.L: _____ % OF ACCOUNT: _____ USD VALUE: _____

CRYPTO
TRADING LOG BOOK

TRADING DETAILS

○ BUY ○ PROFIT DATE TIME: ENTRY PRICE: PAIR:
○ SELL ○ LOSS   DATE TIME: EXIT PRICE:

MENTAL STATE

EXIT CONDITION

SETUP

NOTES

SATOSH W.L: _____ % OF ACCOUNT: _____ USD VALUE: _____

TRADING DETAILS

○ BUY ○ PROFIT DATE TIME: ENTRY PRICE: PAIR:
○ SELL ○ LOSS   DATE TIME: EXIT PRICE:

MENTAL STATE

EXIT CONDITION

SETUP

NOTES

SATOSH W.L: _____ % OF ACCOUNT: _____ USD VALUE: _____

CRYPTO
TRADING LOG BOOK

TRADING DETAILS

○ BUY ○ PROFIT	DATE TIME:	ENTRY PRICE:	PAIR:
○ SELL ○ LOSS	DATE TIME:	EXIT PRICE:	

MENTAL STATE

EXIT CONDITION

SETUP

NOTES

SATOSH W.L: _____ % OF ACCOUNT: _____ USD VALUE: _____

TRADING DETAILS

○ BUY ○ PROFIT	DATE TIME:	ENTRY PRICE:	PAIR:
○ SELL ○ LOSS	DATE TIME:	EXIT PRICE:	

MENTAL STATE

EXIT CONDITION

SETUP

NOTES

SATOSH W.L: _____ % OF ACCOUNT: _____ USD VALUE: _____

CRYPTO
TRADING LOG BOOK

TRADING DETAILS

| ○ BUY ○ PROFIT | DATE TIME: | ENTRY PRICE: | PAIR: |
| ○ SELL ○ LOSS | DATE TIME: | EXIT PRICE: | |

MENTAL STATE

EXIT CONDITION

SETUP

NOTES

SATOSH W.L:_____ % OF ACCOUNT: _____ USD VALUE: _____

TRADING DETAILS

| ○ BUY ○ PROFIT | DATE TIME: | ENTRY PRICE: | PAIR: |
| ○ SELL ○ LOSS | DATE TIME: | EXIT PRICE: | |

MENTAL STATE

EXIT CONDITION

SETUP

NOTES

SATOSH W.L:_____ % OF ACCOUNT: _____ USD VALUE: _____

CRYPTO
TRADING LOG BOOK

TRADING DETAILS

| ○ BUY ○ PROFIT | DATE TIME: | ENTRY PRICE: | PAIR: |
| ○ SELL ○ LOSS | DATE TIME: | EXIT PRICE: | |

MENTAL STATE

EXIT CONDITION

SETUP

NOTES

SATOSH W.L: _____ % OF ACCOUNT: _____ USD VALUE: _____

TRADING DETAILS

| ○ BUY ○ PROFIT | DATE TIME: | ENTRY PRICE: | PAIR: |
| ○ SELL ○ LOSS | DATE TIME: | EXIT PRICE: | |

MENTAL STATE

EXIT CONDITION

SETUP

NOTES

SATOSH W.L: _____ % OF ACCOUNT: _____ USD VALUE: _____

CRYPTO
TRADING LOG BOOK

TRADING DETAILS

○ BUY ○ PROFIT	DATE TIME:	ENTRY PRICE:	PAIR:
○ SELL ○ LOSS	DATE TIME:	EXIT PRICE:	

MENTAL STATE

EXIT CONDITION

SETUP

NOTES

SATOSH W.L:_____ % OF ACCOUNT: _____ USD VALUE: _____

TRADING DETAILS

○ BUY ○ PROFIT	DATE TIME:	ENTRY PRICE:	PAIR:
○ SELL ○ LOSS	DATE TIME:	EXIT PRICE:	

MENTAL STATE

EXIT CONDITION

SETUP

NOTES

SATOSH W.L:_____ % OF ACCOUNT: _____ USD VALUE: _____

CRYPTO
TRADING LOG BOOK

TRADING DETAILS

| ○ BUY   ○ PROFIT | DATE TIME: | ENTRY PRICE: | PAIR: |
| ○ SELL   ○ LOSS | DATE TIME: | EXIT PRICE: | |

MENTRAL STATE

EXIT CONDITION

SETUP

NOTES

SATOSH W.L: _____   % OF ACCOUNT: _____   USD VALUE: _____

TRADING DETAILS

| ○ BUY   ○ PROFIT | DATE TIME: | ENTRY PRICE: | PAIR: |
| ○ SELL   ○ LOSS | DATE TIME: | EXIT PRICE: | |

MENTAL STATE

EXIT CONDITION

SETUP

NOTES

SATOSH W.L: _____   % OF ACCOUNT: _____   USD VALUE: _____

CRYPTO
TRADING LOG BOOK

TRADING DETAILS

| ○ BUY   ○ PROFIT | DATE TIME: | ENTRY PRICE: | PAIR: |
| ○ SELL ○ LOSS | DATE TIME: | EXIT PRICE: | |

MENTAL STATE

EXIT CONDITION

SETUP

NOTES

SATOSH W.L: _____ % OF ACCOUNT: _____ USD VALUE: _____

TRADING DETAILS

| ○ BUY   ○ PROFIT | DATE TIME: | ENTRY PRICE: | PAIR: |
| ○ SELL ○ LOSS | DATE TIME: | EXIT PRICE: | |

MENTAL STATE

EXIT CONDITION

SETUP

NOTES

SATOSH W.L: _____ % OF ACCOUNT: _____ USD VALUE: _____

CRYPTO
TRADING LOG BOOK

TRADING DETAILS

| ○ BUY   ○ PROFIT | DATE TIME: | ENTRY PRICE: | PAIR: |
| ○ SELL ○ LOSS | DATE TIME: | EXIT PRICE: | |

MENTAL STATE

EXIT CONDITION

SETUP

NOTES

SATOSH W.L: _____ % OF ACCOUNT: _____ USD VALUE: _____

TRADING DETAILS

| ○ BUY   ○ PROFIT | DATE TIME: | ENTRY PRICE: | PAIR: |
| ○ SELL ○ LOSS | DATE TIME: | EXIT PRICE: | |

MENTAL STATE

EXIT CONDITION

SETUP

NOTES

SATOSH W.L: _____ % OF ACCOUNT: _____ USD VALUE: _____

CRYPTO
TRADING LOG BOOK

TRADING DETAILS

| ○ BUY ○ PROFIT | DATE TIME: | ENTRY PRICE: | PAIR: |
| ○ SELL ○ LOSS | DATE TIME: | EXIT PRICE: | |

MENTAL STATE

EXIT CONDITION

SETUP

NOTES

SATOSH W.L:_____ % OF ACCOUNT:_____ USD VALUE:_____

TRADING DETAILS

| ○ BUY ○ PROFIT | DATE TIME: | ENTRY PRICE: | PAIR: |
| ○ SELL ○ LOSS | DATE TIME: | EXIT PRICE: | |

MENTAL STATE

EXIT CONDITION

SETUP

NOTES

SATOSH W.L:_____ % OF ACCOUNT:_____ USD VALUE:_____

CRYPTO
TRADING LOG BOOK

TRADING DETAILS

| ○ BUY ○ PROFIT | DATE TIME: | ENTRY PRICE: | PAIR: |
| ○ SELL ○ LOSS | DATE TIME: | EXIT PRICE: | |

MENTAL STATE

EXIT CONDITION

SETUP

NOTES

SATOSH W.L:_____ % OF ACCOUNT: _____ USD VALUE: _____

TRADING DETAILS

| ○ BUY ○ PROFIT | DATE TIME: | ENTRY PRICE: | PAIR: |
| ○ SELL ○ LOSS | DATE TIME: | EXIT PRICE: | |

MENTAL STATE

EXIT CONDITION

SETUP

NOTES

SATOSH W.L:_____ % OF ACCOUNT: _____ USD VALUE: _____

CRYPTO
TRADING LOG BOOK

TRADING DETAILS

| ○ BUY ○ PROFIT | DATE TIME: | ENTRY PRICE: | PAIR: |
| ○ SELL ○ LOSS | DATE TIME: | EXIT PRICE: | |

MENTAL STATE

EXIT CONDITION

SETUP

NOTES

SATOSH W.L:_____ % OF ACCOUNT:_____ USD VALUE:_____

TRADING DETAILS

| ○ BUY ○ PROFIT | DATE TIME: | ENTRY PRICE: | PAIR: |
| ○ SELL ○ LOSS | DATE TIME: | EXIT PRICE: | |

MENTAL STATE

EXIT CONDITION

SETUP

NOTES

SATOSH W.L:_____ % OF ACCOUNT:_____ USD VALUE:_____

CRYPTO
TRADING LOG BOOK

TRADING DETAILS

○ BUY ○ PROFIT	DATE TIME:	ENTRY PRICE:	PAIR:
○ SELL ○ LOSS	DATE TIME:	EXIT PRICE:	

MENTAL STATE

EXIT CONDITION

SETUP

NOTES

SATOSH W.L:_____ % OF ACCOUNT:_____ USD VALUE:_____

TRADING DETAILS

○ BUY ○ PROFIT	DATE TIME:	ENTRY PRICE:	PAIR:
○ SELL ○ LOSS	DATE TIME:	EXIT PRICE:	

MENTAL STATE

EXIT CONDITION

SETUP

NOTES

SATOSH W.L:_____ % OF ACCOUNT:_____ USD VALUE:_____

CRYPTO
TRADING LOG BOOK

TRADING DETAILS

○ BUY ○ PROFIT	DATE TIME:	ENTRY PRICE:	PAIR:
○ SELL ○ LOSS	DATE TIME:	EXIT PRICE:	

MENTAL STATE

EXIT CONDITION

SETUP

NOTES

SATOSH W.L:_____ % OF ACCOUNT:_____ USD VALUE:_____

TRADING DETAILS

○ BUY ○ PROFIT	DATE TIME:	ENTRY PRICE:	PAIR:
○ SELL ○ LOSS	DATE TIME:	EXIT PRICE:	

MENTAL STATE

EXIT CONDITION

SETUP

NOTES

SATOSH W.L:_____ % OF ACCOUNT:_____ USD VALUE:_____

CRYPTO
TRADING LOG BOOK

TRADING DETAILS

| ○ BUY ○ PROFIT | DATE TIME: | ENTRY PRICE: | PAIR: |
| ○ SELL ○ LOSS | DATE TIME: | EXIT PRICE: | |

MENTAL STATE

EXIT CONDITION

SETUP

NOTES

SATOSH W.L: _____ % OF ACCOUNT: _____ USD VALUE: _____

TRADING DETAILS

| ○ BUY ○ PROFIT | DATE TIME: | ENTRY PRICE: | PAIR: |
| ○ SELL ○ LOSS | DATE TIME: | EXIT PRICE: | |

MENTAL STATE

EXIT CONDITION

SETUP

NOTES

SATOSH W.L: _____ % OF ACCOUNT: _____ USD VALUE: _____

CRYPTO
TRADING LOG BOOK

TRADING DETAILS

| ○ BUY   ○ PROFIT | DATE TIME: | ENTRY PRICE: | PAIR: |
| ○ SELL ○ LOSS | DATE TIME: | EXIT PRICE: | |

MENTAL STATE

EXIT CONDITION

SETUP

NOTES

SATOSH W.L:_____ % OF ACCOUNT: _____ USD VALUE: _____

TRADING DETAILS

| ○ BUY   ○ PROFIT | DATE TIME: | ENTRY PRICE: | PAIR: |
| ○ SELL ○ LOSS | DATE TIME: | EXIT PRICE: | |

MENTAL STATE

EXIT CONDITION

SETUP

NOTES

SATOSH W.L:_____ % OF ACCOUNT: _____ USD VALUE: _____

CRYPTO
TRADING LOG BOOK

TRADING DETAILS

| ○ BUY   ○ PROFIT | DATE TIME: | ENTRY PRICE: | PAIR: |
| ○ SELL ○ LOSS | DATE TIME: | EXIT PRICE: | |

MENTAL STATE

EXIT CONDITION

SETUP

NOTES

SATOSH W.L: _____ % OF ACCOUNT: _____ USD VALUE: _____

TRADING DETAILS

| ○ BUY   ○ PROFIT | DATE TIME: | ENTRY PRICE: | PAIR: |
| ○ SELL ○ LOSS | DATE TIME: | EXIT PRICE: | |

MENTAL STATE

EXIT CONDITION

SETUP

NOTES

SATOSH W.L: _____ % OF ACCOUNT: _____ USD VALUE: _____

CRYPTO
TRADING LOG BOOK

TRADING DETAILS

| ○ BUY ○ PROFIT | DATE TIME: | ENTRY PRICE: | PAIR: |
| ○ SELL ○ LOSS | DATE TIME: | EXIT PRICE: | |

MENTAL STATE

EXIT CONDITION

SETUP

NOTES

SATOSH W.L:_____ % OF ACCOUNT:_____ USD VALUE:_____

TRADING DETAILS

| ○ BUY ○ PROFIT | DATE TIME: | ENTRY PRICE: | PAIR: |
| ○ SELL ○ LOSS | DATE TIME: | EXIT PRICE: | |

MENTAL STATE

EXIT CONDITION

SETUP

NOTES

SATOSH W.L:_____ % OF ACCOUNT:_____ USD VALUE:_____

CRYPTO
TRADING LOG BOOK

TRADING DETAILS

○ BUY ○ PROFIT	DATE TIME:	ENTRY PRICE:	PAIR:
○ SELL ○ LOSS	DATE TIME:	EXIT PRICE:	

MENTAL STATE

EXIT CONDITION

SETUP

NOTES

SATOSH W.L: _____ % OF ACCOUNT: _____ USD VALUE: _____

TRADING DETAILS

○ BUY ○ PROFIT	DATE TIME:	ENTRY PRICE:	PAIR:
○ SELL ○ LOSS	DATE TIME:	EXIT PRICE:	

MENTAL STATE

EXIT CONDITION

SETUP

NOTES

SATOSH W.L: _____ % OF ACCOUNT: _____ USD VALUE: _____

CRYPTO
TRADING LOG BOOK

TRADING DETAILS

◯ BUY ◯ PROFIT	DATE TIME:	ENTRY PRICE:	PAIR:
◯ SELL ◯ LOSS	DATE TIME:	EXIT PRICE:	

MENTRAL STATE / EXIT CONDITION

SETUP / NOTES

SATOSH W.L:_____ % OF ACCOUNT:_____ USD VALUE:_____

TRADING DETAILS

◯ BUY ◯ PROFIT	DATE TIME:	ENTRY PRICE:	PAIR:
◯ SELL ◯ LOSS	DATE TIME:	EXIT PRICE:	

MENTAL STATE / EXIT CONDITION

SETUP / NOTES

SATOSH W.L:_____ % OF ACCOUNT:_____ USD VALUE:_____

CRYPTO
TRADING LOG BOOK

TRADING DETAILS

○ BUY ○ PROFIT DATE TIME:

○ SELL ○ LOSS DATE TIME:

ENTRY PRICE:

EXIT PRICE:

PAIR:

MENTAL STATE

EXIT CONDITION

SETUP

NOTES

SATOSH W.L:_____ % OF ACCOUNT:_____ USD VALUE:_____

TRADING DETAILS

○ BUY ○ PROFIT DATE TIME:

○ SELL ○ LOSS DATE TIME:

ENTRY PRICE:

EXIT PRICE:

PAIR:

MENTAL STATE

EXIT CONDITION

SETUP

NOTES

SATOSH W.L:_____ % OF ACCOUNT:_____ USD VALUE:_____

CRYPTO
TRADING LOG BOOK

TRADING DETAILS

| ○ BUY ○ PROFIT | DATE TIME: | ENTRY PRICE: | PAIR: |
| ○ SELL ○ LOSS | DATE TIME: | EXIT PRICE: | |

MENTAL STATE

EXIT CONDITION

SETUP

NOTES

SATOSH W.L:_____ % OF ACCOUNT:_____ USD VALUE:_____

TRADING DETAILS

| ○ BUY ○ PROFIT | DATE TIME: | ENTRY PRICE: | PAIR: |
| ○ SELL ○ LOSS | DATE TIME: | EXIT PRICE: | |

MENTAL STATE

EXIT CONDITION

SETUP

NOTES

SATOSH W.L:_____ % OF ACCOUNT:_____ USD VALUE:_____

CRYPTO
TRADING LOG BOOK

TRADING DETAILS

| ○ BUY   ○ PROFIT | DATE TIME: | ENTRY PRICE: | PAIR: |
| ○ SELL ○ LOSS | DATE TIME: | EXIT PRICE: | |

MENTAL STATE

EXIT CONDITION

SETUP

NOTES

SATOSH W.L: _____ % OF ACCOUNT: _____ USD VALUE: _____

TRADING DETAILS

| ○ BUY   ○ PROFIT | DATE TIME: | ENTRY PRICE: | PAIR: |
| ○ SELL ○ LOSS | DATE TIME: | EXIT PRICE: | |

MENTAL STATE

EXIT CONDITION

SETUP

NOTES

SATOSH W.L: _____ % OF ACCOUNT: _____ USD VALUE: _____

CRYPTO
TRADING LOG BOOK

TRADING DETAILS

○ BUY ○ PROFIT	DATE TIME:	ENTRY PRICE:	PAIR:
○ SELL ○ LOSS	DATE TIME:	EXIT PRICE:	

MENTAL STATE

EXIT CONDITION

SETUP

NOTES

SATOSH W.L: _____ % OF ACCOUNT: _____ USD VALUE: _____

TRADING DETAILS

○ BUY ○ PROFIT	DATE TIME:	ENTRY PRICE:	PAIR:
○ SELL ○ LOSS	DATE TIME:	EXIT PRICE:	

MENTAL STATE

EXIT CONDITION

SETUP

NOTES

SATOSH W.L: _____ % OF ACCOUNT: _____ USD VALUE: _____

CRYPTO
TRADING LOG BOOK

TRADING DETAILS

| ○ BUY ○ PROFIT | DATE TIME: | ENTRY PRICE: | PAIR: |
| ○ SELL ○ LOSS | DATE TIME: | EXIT PRICE: | |

MENTAL STATE

EXIT CONDITION

SETUP

NOTES

SATOSH W.L:_____ % OF ACCOUNT: _____ USD VALUE: _____

TRADING DETAILS

| ○ BUY ○ PROFIT | DATE TIME: | ENTRY PRICE: | PAIR: |
| ○ SELL ○ LOSS | DATE TIME: | EXIT PRICE: | |

MENTAL STATE

EXIT CONDITION

SETUP

NOTES

SATOSH W.L:_____ % OF ACCOUNT: _____ USD VALUE: _____

CRYPTO
TRADING LOG BOOK

TRADING DETAILS

○ BUY ○ PROFIT DATE TIME: ENTRY PRICE: PAIR:

○ SELL ○ LOSS   DATE TIME: EXIT PRICE:

MENTRAL STATE   EXIT CONDITION

SETUP   NOTES

SATOSH W.L:_____ % OF ACCOUNT:_____ USD VALUE:_____

TRADING DETAILS

○ BUY ○ PROFIT DATE TIME: ENTRY PRICE: PAIR:

○ SELL ○ LOSS   DATE TIME: EXIT PRICE:

MENTAL STATE   EXIT CONDITION

SETUP   NOTES

SATOSH W.L:_____ % OF ACCOUNT:_____ USD VALUE:_____

CRYPTO
TRADING LOG BOOK

TRADING DETAILS

○ BUY ○ PROFIT	DATE TIME:	ENTRY PRICE:	PAIR:
○ SELL ○ LOSS	DATE TIME:	EXIT PRICE:	

MENTAL STATE

EXIT CONDITION

SETUP

NOTES

SATOSH W.L:_____ % OF ACCOUNT: _____ USD VALUE: _____

TRADING DETAILS

○ BUY ○ PROFIT	DATE TIME:	ENTRY PRICE:	PAIR:
○ SELL ○ LOSS	DATE TIME:	EXIT PRICE:	

MENTAL STATE

EXIT CONDITION

SETUP

NOTES

SATOSH W.L:_____ % OF ACCOUNT: _____ USD VALUE: _____

CRYPTO
TRADING LOG BOOK

TRADING DETAILS

| ○ BUY ○ PROFIT | DATE TIME: | ENTRY PRICE: | PAIR: |
| ○ SELL ○ LOSS | DATE TIME: | EXIT PRICE: | |

MENTAL STATE

EXIT CONDITION

SETUP

NOTES

SATOSH W.L:_____ % OF ACCOUNT:_____ USD VALUE:_____

TRADING DETAILS

| ○ BUY ○ PROFIT | DATE TIME: | ENTRY PRICE: | PAIR: |
| ○ SELL ○ LOSS | DATE TIME: | EXIT PRICE: | |

MENTAL STATE

EXIT CONDITION

SETUP

NOTES

SATOSH W.L:_____ % OF ACCOUNT:_____ USD VALUE:_____

CRYPTO
TRADING LOG BOOK

TRADING DETAILS

○ BUY ○ PROFIT	DATE TIME:	ENTRY PRICE:	PAIR:
○ SELL ○ LOSS	DATE TIME:	EXIT PRICE:	

MENTAL STATE

EXIT CONDITION

SETUP

NOTES

SATOSH W.L: _____ % OF ACCOUNT: _____ USD VALUE: _____

TRADING DETAILS

○ BUY ○ PROFIT	DATE TIME:	ENTRY PRICE:	PAIR:
○ SELL ○ LOSS	DATE TIME:	EXIT PRICE:	

MENTAL STATE

EXIT CONDITION

SETUP

NOTES

SATOSH W.L: _____ % OF ACCOUNT: _____ USD VALUE: _____

CRYPTO
TRADING LOG BOOK

TRADING DETAILS

| ○ BUY   ○ PROFIT | DATE TIME: | ENTRY PRICE: | PAIR: |
| ○ SELL ○ LOSS | DATE TIME: | EXIT PRICE: | |

MENTAL STATE

EXIT CONDITION

SETUP

NOTES

SATOSH W.L: _____ % OF ACCOUNT: _____ USD VALUE: _____

TRADING DETAILS

| ○ BUY   ○ PROFIT | DATE TIME: | ENTRY PRICE: | PAIR: |
| ○ SELL ○ LOSS | DATE TIME: | EXIT PRICE: | |

MENTAL STATE

EXIT CONDITION

SETUP

NOTES

SATOSH W.L: _____ % OF ACCOUNT: _____ USD VALUE: _____

CRYPTO
TRADING LOG BOOK

TRADING DETAILS

| ○ BUY ○ PROFIT | DATE TIME: | ENTRY PRICE: | PAIR: |
| ○ SELL ○ LOSS | DATE TIME: | EXIT PRICE: | |

MENTAL STATE

EXIT CONDITION

SETUP

NOTES

SATOSH W.L:_____ % OF ACCOUNT:_____ USD VALUE:_____

TRADING DETAILS

| ○ BUY ○ PROFIT | DATE TIME: | ENTRY PRICE: | PAIR: |
| ○ SELL ○ LOSS | DATE TIME: | EXIT PRICE: | |

MENTAL STATE

EXIT CONDITION

SETUP

NOTES

SATOSH W.L:_____ % OF ACCOUNT:_____ USD VALUE:_____

CRYPTO
TRADING LOG BOOK

TRADING DETAILS

○ BUY ○ PROFIT DATE TIME: | ENTRY PRICE: | PAIR:
○ SELL ○ LOSS   DATE TIME: | EXIT PRICE: |

MENTAL STATE

EXIT CONDITION

SETUP

NOTES

SATOSH W.L:_____ % OF ACCOUNT:_____ USD VALUE:_____

TRADING DETAILS

○ BUY ○ PROFIT DATE TIME: | ENTRY PRICE: | PAIR:
○ SELL ○ LOSS   DATE TIME: | EXIT PRICE: |

MENTAL STATE

EXIT CONDITION

SETUP

NOTES

SATOSH W.L:_____ % OF ACCOUNT:_____ USD VALUE:_____

CRYPTO
TRADING LOG BOOK

TRADING DETAILS

| ○ BUY ○ PROFIT | DATE TIME: | ENTRY PRICE: | PAIR: |
| ○ SELL ○ LOSS | DATE TIME: | EXIT PRICE: | |

MENTAL STATE

EXIT CONDITION

SETUP

NOTES

SATOSH W.L:_____ % OF ACCOUNT: _____ USD VALUE: _____

TRADING DETAILS

| ○ BUY ○ PROFIT | DATE TIME: | ENTRY PRICE: | PAIR: |
| ○ SELL ○ LOSS | DATE TIME: | EXIT PRICE: | |

MENTAL STATE

EXIT CONDITION

SETUP

NOTES

SATOSH W.L:_____ % OF ACCOUNT: _____ USD VALUE: _____

CRYPTO
TRADING LOG BOOK

TRADING DETAILS

○ BUY ○ PROFIT	DATE TIME:	ENTRY PRICE:	PAIR:
○ SELL ○ LOSS	DATE TIME:	EXIT PRICE:	

MENTAL STATE

EXIT CONDITION

SETUP

NOTES

SATOSH W.L:_____ % OF ACCOUNT:_____ USD VALUE:_____

TRADING DETAILS

○ BUY ○ PROFIT	DATE TIME:	ENTRY PRICE:	PAIR:
○ SELL ○ LOSS	DATE TIME:	EXIT PRICE:	

MENTAL STATE

EXIT CONDITION

SETUP

NOTES

SATOSH W.L:_____ % OF ACCOUNT:_____ USD VALUE:_____

CRYPTO
TRADING LOG BOOK

TRADING DETAILS

| ○ BUY ○ PROFIT | DATE TIME: | ENTRY PRICE: | PAIR: |
| ○ SELL ○ LOSS | DATE TIME: | EXIT PRICE: | |

MENTAL STATE

EXIT CONDITION

SETUP

NOTES

SATOSH W.L:_____ % OF ACCOUNT:_____ USD VALUE:_____

TRADING DETAILS

| ○ BUY ○ PROFIT | DATE TIME: | ENTRY PRICE: | PAIR: |
| ○ SELL ○ LOSS | DATE TIME: | EXIT PRICE: | |

MENTAL STATE

EXIT CONDITION

SETUP

NOTES

SATOSH W.L:_____ % OF ACCOUNT:_____ USD VALUE:_____

CRYPTO
TRADING LOG BOOK

TRADING DETAILS

○ BUY ○ PROFIT	DATE TIME:	ENTRY PRICE:	PAIR:
○ SELL ○ LOSS	DATE TIME:	EXIT PRICE:	

MENTAL STATE

EXIT CONDITION

SETUP

NOTES

SATOSH W.L:_____ % OF ACCOUNT:_____ USD VALUE:_____

TRADING DETAILS

○ BUY ○ PROFIT	DATE TIME:	ENTRY PRICE:	PAIR:
○ SELL ○ LOSS	DATE TIME:	EXIT PRICE:	

MENTAL STATE

EXIT CONDITION

SETUP

NOTES

SATOSH W.L:_____ % OF ACCOUNT:_____ USD VALUE:_____

CRYPTO
TRADING LOG BOOK

TRADING DETAILS

| ○ BUY   ○ PROFIT | DATE TIME: | ENTRY PRICE: | PAIR: |
| ○ SELL ○ LOSS | DATE TIME: | EXIT PRICE: | |

MENTAL STATE

EXIT CONDITION

SETUP

NOTES

SATOSH W.L: _____ % OF ACCOUNT: _____ USD VALUE: _____

TRADING DETAILS

| ○ BUY   ○ PROFIT | DATE TIME: | ENTRY PRICE: | PAIR: |
| ○ SELL ○ LOSS | DATE TIME: | EXIT PRICE: | |

MENTAL STATE

EXIT CONDITION

SETUP

NOTES

SATOSH W.L: _____ % OF ACCOUNT: _____ USD VALUE: _____

CRYPTO
TRADING LOG BOOK

TRADING DETAILS

| ○ BUY ○ PROFIT | DATE TIME: | ENTRY PRICE: | PAIR: |
| ○ SELL ○ LOSS | DATE TIME: | EXIT PRICE: | |

MENTAL STATE

EXIT CONDITION

SETUP

NOTES

SATOSH W.L:_____ % OF ACCOUNT:_____ USD VALUE:_____

TRADING DETAILS

| ○ BUY ○ PROFIT | DATE TIME: | ENTRY PRICE: | PAIR: |
| ○ SELL ○ LOSS | DATE TIME: | EXIT PRICE: | |

MENTAL STATE

EXIT CONDITION

SETUP

NOTES

SATOSH W.L:_____ % OF ACCOUNT:_____ USD VALUE:_____

CRYPTO
TRADING LOG BOOK

TRADING DETAILS

| ○ BUY ○ PROFIT | DATE TIME: | ENTRY PRICE: | PAIR: |
| ○ SELL ○ LOSS | DATE TIME: | EXIT PRICE: | |

MENTAL STATE

EXIT CONDITION

SETUP

NOTES

SATOSH W.L:_____ % OF ACCOUNT:_____ USD VALUE:_____

TRADING DETAILS

| ○ BUY ○ PROFIT | DATE TIME: | ENTRY PRICE: | PAIR: |
| ○ SELL ○ LOSS | DATE TIME: | EXIT PRICE: | |

MENTAL STATE

EXIT CONDITION

SETUP

NOTES

SATOSH W.L:_____ % OF ACCOUNT:_____ USD VALUE:_____

CRYPTO
TRADING LOG BOOK

TRADING DETAILS

| ○ BUY ○ PROFIT | DATE TIME: | ENTRY PRICE: | PAIR: |
| ○ SELL ○ LOSS | DATE TIME: | EXIT PRICE: | |

MENTAL STATE

EXIT CONDITION

SETUP

NOTES

SATOSH W.L:_____ % OF ACCOUNT:_____ USD VALUE:_____

TRADING DETAILS

| ○ BUY ○ PROFIT | DATE TIME: | ENTRY PRICE: | PAIR: |
| ○ SELL ○ LOSS | DATE TIME: | EXIT PRICE: | |

MENTAL STATE

EXIT CONDITION

SETUP

NOTES

SATOSH W.L:_____ % OF ACCOUNT:_____ USD VALUE:_____

CRYPTO
TRADING LOG BOOK

TRADING DETAILS

| ○ BUY ○ PROFIT | DATE TIME: | ENTRY PRICE: | PAIR: |
| ○ SELL ○ LOSS | DATE TIME: | EXIT PRICE: | |

MENTAL STATE

EXIT CONDITION

SETUP

NOTES

SATOSH W.L:_____ % OF ACCOUNT:_____ USD VALUE:_____

TRADING DETAILS

| ○ BUY ○ PROFIT | DATE TIME: | ENTRY PRICE: | PAIR: |
| ○ SELL ○ LOSS | DATE TIME: | EXIT PRICE: | |

MENTAL STATE

EXIT CONDITION

SETUP

NOTES

SATOSH W.L:_____ % OF ACCOUNT:_____ USD VALUE:_____

CRYPTO
TRADING LOG BOOK

TRADING DETAILS

| ○ BUY ○ PROFIT | DATE TIME: | ENTRY PRICE: | PAIR: |
| ○ SELL ○ LOSS | DATE TIME: | EXIT PRICE: | |

MENTAL STATE

EXIT CONDITION

SETUP

NOTES

SATOSH W.L: _____ % OF ACCOUNT: _____ USD VALUE: _____

TRADING DETAILS

| ○ BUY ○ PROFIT | DATE TIME: | ENTRY PRICE: | PAIR: |
| ○ SELL ○ LOSS | DATE TIME: | EXIT PRICE: | |

MENTAL STATE

EXIT CONDITION

SETUP

NOTES

SATOSH W.L: _____ % OF ACCOUNT: _____ USD VALUE: _____

CRYPTO
TRADING LOG BOOK

TRADING DETAILS

○ BUY ○ PROFIT	DATE TIME:	ENTRY PRICE:	PAIR:
○ SELL ○ LOSS	DATE TIME:	EXIT PRICE:	

MENTAL STATE

EXIT CONDITION

SETUP

NOTES

SATOSH W.L: _____ % OF ACCOUNT: _____ USD VALUE: _____

TRADING DETAILS

○ BUY ○ PROFIT	DATE TIME:	ENTRY PRICE:	PAIR:
○ SELL ○ LOSS	DATE TIME:	EXIT PRICE:	

MENTAL STATE

EXIT CONDITION

SETUP

NOTES

SATOSH W.L: _____ % OF ACCOUNT: _____ USD VALUE: _____

CRYPTO
TRADING LOG BOOK

TRADING DETAILS

| ○ BUY ○ PROFIT | DATE TIME: | ENTRY PRICE: | PAIR: |
| ○ SELL ○ LOSS | DATE TIME: | EXIT PRICE: | |

MENTAL STATE

EXIT CONDITION

SETUP

NOTES

SATOSH W.L: _____ % OF ACCOUNT: _____ USD VALUE: _____

TRADING DETAILS

| ○ BUY ○ PROFIT | DATE TIME: | ENTRY PRICE: | PAIR: |
| ○ SELL ○ LOSS | DATE TIME: | EXIT PRICE: | |

MENTAL STATE

EXIT CONDITION

SETUP

NOTES

SATOSH W.L: _____ % OF ACCOUNT: _____ USD VALUE: _____

CRYPTO
TRADING LOG BOOK

TRADING DETAILS

○ BUY ○ PROFIT	DATE TIME:	ENTRY PRICE:	PAIR:
○ SELL ○ LOSS	DATE TIME:	EXIT PRICE:	

MENTAL STATE

EXIT CONDITION

SETUP

NOTES

SATOSH W.L:_____ % OF ACCOUNT:_____ USD VALUE:_____

TRADING DETAILS

○ BUY ○ PROFIT	DATE TIME:	ENTRY PRICE:	PAIR:
○ SELL ○ LOSS	DATE TIME:	EXIT PRICE:	

MENTAL STATE

EXIT CONDITION

SETUP

NOTES

SATOSH W.L:_____ % OF ACCOUNT:_____ USD VALUE:_____

CRYPTO
TRADING LOG BOOK

TRADING DETAILS

○ BUY ○ PROFIT	DATE TIME:	ENTRY PRICE:	PAIR:
○ SELL ○ LOSS	DATE TIME:	EXIT PRICE:	

MENTAL STATE

EXIT CONDITION

SETUP

NOTES

SATOSH W.L:_____ % OF ACCOUNT:_____ USD VALUE:_____

TRADING DETAILS

○ BUY ○ PROFIT	DATE TIME:	ENTRY PRICE:	PAIR:
○ SELL ○ LOSS	DATE TIME:	EXIT PRICE:	

MENTAL STATE

EXIT CONDITION

SETUP

NOTES

SATOSH W.L:_____ % OF ACCOUNT:_____ USD VALUE:_____

CRYPTO
TRADING LOG BOOK

TRADING DETAILS

| ○ BUY ○ PROFIT | DATE TIME: | ENTRY PRICE: | PAIR: |
| ○ SELL ○ LOSS | DATE TIME: | EXIT PRICE: | |

MENTAL STATE

EXIT CONDITION

SETUP

NOTES

SATOSH W.L:_____ % OF ACCOUNT:_____ USD VALUE:_____

TRADING DETAILS

| ○ BUY ○ PROFIT | DATE TIME: | ENTRY PRICE: | PAIR: |
| ○ SELL ○ LOSS | DATE TIME: | EXIT PRICE: | |

MENTAL STATE

EXIT CONDITION

SETUP

NOTES

SATOSH W.L:_____ % OF ACCOUNT:_____ USD VALUE:_____

CRYPTO
TRADING LOG BOOK

TRADING DETAILS

| ○ BUY ○ PROFIT | DATE TIME: | ENTRY PRICE: | PAIR: |
| ○ SELL ○ LOSS | DATE TIME: | EXIT PRICE: | |

MENTAL STATE

EXIT CONDITION

SETUP

NOTES

SATOSH W.L:_____ % OF ACCOUNT:_____ USD VALUE:_____

TRADING DETAILS

| ○ BUY ○ PROFIT | DATE TIME: | ENTRY PRICE: | PAIR: |
| ○ SELL ○ LOSS | DATE TIME: | EXIT PRICE: | |

MENTAL STATE

EXIT CONDITION

SETUP

NOTES

SATOSH W.L:_____ % OF ACCOUNT:_____ USD VALUE:_____

CRYPTO
TRADING LOG BOOK

TRADING DETAILS

| ○ BUY ○ PROFIT | DATE TIME: | ENTRY PRICE: | PAIR: |
| ○ SELL ○ LOSS | DATE TIME: | EXIT PRICE: | |

MENTAL STATE

EXIT CONDITION

SETUP

NOTES

SATOSH W.L: _____ % OF ACCOUNT: _____ USD VALUE: _____

TRADING DETAILS

| ○ BUY ○ PROFIT | DATE TIME: | ENTRY PRICE: | PAIR: |
| ○ SELL ○ LOSS | DATE TIME: | EXIT PRICE: | |

MENTAL STATE

EXIT CONDITION

SETUP

NOTES

SATOSH W.L: _____ % OF ACCOUNT: _____ USD VALUE: _____

CRYPTO
TRADING LOG BOOK

TRADING DETAILS

| ○ BUY ○ PROFIT | DATE TIME: | ENTRY PRICE: | PAIR: |
| ○ SELL ○ LOSS | DATE TIME: | EXIT PRICE: | |

MENTAL STATE

EXIT CONDITION

SETUP

NOTES

SATOSH W.L:_____ % OF ACCOUNT: _____ USD VALUE: _____

TRADING DETAILS

| ○ BUY ○ PROFIT | DATE TIME: | ENTRY PRICE: | PAIR: |
| ○ SELL ○ LOSS | DATE TIME: | EXIT PRICE: | |

MENTAL STATE

EXIT CONDITION

SETUP

NOTES

SATOSH W.L:_____ % OF ACCOUNT: _____ USD VALUE: _____

CRYPTO
TRADING LOG BOOK

TRADING DETAILS

| ○ BUY ○ PROFIT | DATE TIME: | ENTRY PRICE: | PAIR: |
| ○ SELL ○ LOSS | DATE TIME: | EXIT PRICE: | |

MENTAL STATE

EXIT CONDITION

SETUP

NOTES

SATOSH W.L: _____ % OF ACCOUNT: _____ USD VALUE: _____

TRADING DETAILS

| ○ BUY ○ PROFIT | DATE TIME: | ENTRY PRICE: | PAIR: |
| ○ SELL ○ LOSS | DATE TIME: | EXIT PRICE: | |

MENTAL STATE

EXIT CONDITION

SETUP

NOTES

SATOSH W.L: _____ % OF ACCOUNT: _____ USD VALUE: _____

CRYPTO
TRADING LOG BOOK

TRADING DETAILS

| ○ BUY ○ PROFIT | DATE TIME: | ENTRY PRICE: | PAIR: |
| ○ SELL ○ LOSS | DATE TIME: | EXIT PRICE: | |

MENTAL STATE

EXIT CONDITION

SETUP

NOTES

SATOSH W.L:_____ % OF ACCOUNT:_____ USD VALUE:_____

TRADING DETAILS

| ○ BUY ○ PROFIT | DATE TIME: | ENTRY PRICE: | PAIR: |
| ○ SELL ○ LOSS | DATE TIME: | EXIT PRICE: | |

MENTAL STATE

EXIT CONDITION

SETUP

NOTES

SATOSH W.L:_____ % OF ACCOUNT:_____ USD VALUE:_____

CRYPTO
TRADING LOG BOOK

TRADING DETAILS

| ○ BUY ○ PROFIT | DATE TIME: | ENTRY PRICE: | PAIR: |
| ○ SELL ○ LOSS | DATE TIME: | EXIT PRICE: | |

MENTAL STATE

EXIT CONDITION

SETUP

NOTES

SATOSH W.L:_____ % OF ACCOUNT:_____ USD VALUE:_____

TRADING DETAILS

| ○ BUY ○ PROFIT | DATE TIME: | ENTRY PRICE: | PAIR: |
| ○ SELL ○ LOSS | DATE TIME: | EXIT PRICE: | |

MENTAL STATE

EXIT CONDITION

SETUP

NOTES

SATOSH W.L:_____ % OF ACCOUNT:_____ USD VALUE:_____

CRYPTO
TRADING LOG BOOK

TRADING DETAILS

○ BUY ○ PROFIT	DATE TIME:	ENTRY PRICE:	PAIR:
○ SELL ○ LOSS	DATE TIME:	EXIT PRICE:	

MENTAL STATE

EXIT CONDITION

SETUP

NOTES

SATOSH W.L: _____ % OF ACCOUNT: _____ USD VALUE: _____

TRADING DETAILS

○ BUY ○ PROFIT	DATE TIME:	ENTRY PRICE:	PAIR:
○ SELL ○ LOSS	DATE TIME:	EXIT PRICE:	

MENTAL STATE

EXIT CONDITION

SETUP

NOTES

SATOSH W.L: _____ % OF ACCOUNT: _____ USD VALUE: _____

CRYPTO
TRADING LOG BOOK

TRADING DETAILS

| ○ BUY ○ PROFIT | DATE TIME: | ENTRY PRICE: | PAIR: |
| ○ SELL ○ LOSS | DATE TIME: | EXIT PRICE: | |

MENTAL STATE

EXIT CONDITION

SETUP

NOTES

SATOSH W.L:_____ % OF ACCOUNT:_____ USD VALUE:_____

TRADING DETAILS

| ○ BUY ○ PROFIT | DATE TIME: | ENTRY PRICE: | PAIR: |
| ○ SELL ○ LOSS | DATE TIME: | EXIT PRICE: | |

MENTAL STATE

EXIT CONDITION

SETUP

NOTES

SATOSH W.L:_____ % OF ACCOUNT:_____ USD VALUE:_____

CRYPTO
TRADING LOG BOOK

TRADING DETAILS

○ BUY ○ PROFIT	DATE TIME:	ENTRY PRICE:	PAIR:
○ SELL ○ LOSS	DATE TIME:	EXIT PRICE:	

MENTAL STATE

EXIT CONDITION

SETUP

NOTES

SATOSH W.L:_____ % OF ACCOUNT:_____ USD VALUE:_____

TRADING DETAILS

○ BUY ○ PROFIT	DATE TIME:	ENTRY PRICE:	PAIR:
○ SELL ○ LOSS	DATE TIME:	EXIT PRICE:	

MENTAL STATE

EXIT CONDITION

SETUP

NOTES

SATOSH W.L:_____ % OF ACCOUNT:_____ USD VALUE:_____

CRYPTO
TRADING LOG BOOK

TRADING DETAILS

| ○ BUY   ○ PROFIT | DATE TIME: | ENTRY PRICE: | PAIR: |
| ○ SELL ○ LOSS | DATE TIME: | EXIT PRICE: | |

MENTAL STATE

EXIT CONDITION

SETUP

NOTES

SATOSH W.L: _____ % OF ACCOUNT: _____ USD VALUE: _____

TRADING DETAILS

| ○ BUY   ○ PROFIT | DATE TIME: | ENTRY PRICE: | PAIR: |
| ○ SELL ○ LOSS | DATE TIME: | EXIT PRICE: | |

MENTAL STATE

EXIT CONDITION

SETUP

NOTES

SATOSH W.L: _____ % OF ACCOUNT: _____ USD VALUE: _____

CRYPTO
TRADING LOG BOOK

TRADING DETAILS

| ○ BUY ○ PROFIT | DATE TIME: | ENTRY PRICE: | PAIR: |
| ○ SELL ○ LOSS | DATE TIME: | EXIT PRICE: | |

MENTAL STATE

EXIT CONDITION

SETUP

NOTES

SATOSH W.L: _____ % OF ACCOUNT: _____ USD VALUE: _____

TRADING DETAILS

| ○ BUY ○ PROFIT | DATE TIME: | ENTRY PRICE: | PAIR: |
| ○ SELL ○ LOSS | DATE TIME: | EXIT PRICE: | |

MENTAL STATE

EXIT CONDITION

SETUP

NOTES

SATOSH W.L: _____ % OF ACCOUNT: _____ USD VALUE: _____

CRYPTO
TRADING LOG BOOK

TRADING DETAILS

| ○ BUY ○ PROFIT | DATE TIME: | ENTRY PRICE: | PAIR: |
| ○ SELL ○ LOSS | DATE TIME: | EXIT PRICE: | |

MENTAL STATE

EXIT CONDITION

SETUP

NOTES

SATOSH W.L: _____ % OF ACCOUNT: _____ USD VALUE: _____

TRADING DETAILS

| ○ BUY ○ PROFIT | DATE TIME: | ENTRY PRICE: | PAIR: |
| ○ SELL ○ LOSS | DATE TIME: | EXIT PRICE: | |

MENTAL STATE

EXIT CONDITION

SETUP

NOTES

SATOSH W.L: _____ % OF ACCOUNT: _____ USD VALUE: _____

CRYPTO
TRADING LOG BOOK

TRADING DETAILS

| ○ BUY ○ PROFIT | DATE TIME: | ENTRY PRICE: | PAIR: |
| ○ SELL ○ LOSS | DATE TIME: | EXIT PRICE: | |

MENTAL STATE

EXIT CONDITION

SETUP

NOTES

SATOSH W.L: _____ % OF ACCOUNT: _____ USD VALUE: _____

TRADING DETAILS

| ○ BUY ○ PROFIT | DATE TIME: | ENTRY PRICE: | PAIR: |
| ○ SELL ○ LOSS | DATE TIME: | EXIT PRICE: | |

MENTAL STATE

EXIT CONDITION

SETUP

NOTES

SATOSH W.L: _____ % OF ACCOUNT: _____ USD VALUE: _____

CRYPTO
TRADING LOG BOOK

TRADING DETAILS

| ○ BUY   ○ PROFIT | DATE TIME: | ENTRY PRICE: | PAIR: |
| ○ SELL ○ LOSS | DATE TIME: | EXIT PRICE: | |

MENTAL STATE

EXIT CONDITION

SETUP

NOTES

SATOSH W.L: _____ % OF ACCOUNT: _____ USD VALUE: _____

TRADING DETAILS

| ○ BUY   ○ PROFIT | DATE TIME: | ENTRY PRICE: | PAIR: |
| ○ SELL ○ LOSS | DATE TIME: | EXIT PRICE: | |

MENTAL STATE

EXIT CONDITION

SETUP

NOTES

SATOSH W.L: _____ % OF ACCOUNT: _____ USD VALUE: _____

CRYPTO
TRADING LOG BOOK

TRADING DETAILS

| ○ BUY ○ PROFIT | DATE TIME: | ENTRY PRICE: | PAIR: |
| ○ SELL ○ LOSS | DATE TIME: | EXIT PRICE: | |

MENTAL STATE

EXIT CONDITION

SETUP

NOTES

SATOSH W.L: _____ % OF ACCOUNT: _____ USD VALUE: _____

TRADING DETAILS

| ○ BUY ○ PROFIT | DATE TIME: | ENTRY PRICE: | PAIR: |
| ○ SELL ○ LOSS | DATE TIME: | EXIT PRICE: | |

MENTAL STATE

EXIT CONDITION

SETUP

NOTES

SATOSH W.L: _____ % OF ACCOUNT: _____ USD VALUE: _____

CRYPTO
TRADING LOG BOOK

TRADING DETAILS

| ○ BUY ○ PROFIT | DATE TIME: | ENTRY PRICE: | PAIR: |
| ○ SELL ○ LOSS | DATE TIME: | EXIT PRICE: | |

MENTAL STATE

EXIT CONDITION

SETUP

NOTES

SATOSH W.L:_____ % OF ACCOUNT: _____ USD VALUE: _____

TRADING DETAILS

| ○ BUY ○ PROFIT | DATE TIME: | ENTRY PRICE: | PAIR: |
| ○ SELL ○ LOSS | DATE TIME: | EXIT PRICE: | |

MENTAL STATE

EXIT CONDITION

SETUP

NOTES

SATOSH W.L:_____ % OF ACCOUNT: _____ USD VALUE: _____

CRYPTO
TRADING LOG BOOK

TRADING DETAILS

| ○ BUY ○ PROFIT | DATE TIME: | ENTRY PRICE: | PAIR: |
| ○ SELL ○ LOSS | DATE TIME: | EXIT PRICE: | |

MENTAL STATE

EXIT CONDITION

SETUP

NOTES

SATOSH W.L: _____ % OF ACCOUNT: _____ USD VALUE: _____

TRADING DETAILS

| ○ BUY ○ PROFIT | DATE TIME: | ENTRY PRICE: | PAIR: |
| ○ SELL ○ LOSS | DATE TIME: | EXIT PRICE: | |

MENTAL STATE

EXIT CONDITION

SETUP

NOTES

SATOSH W.L: _____ % OF ACCOUNT: _____ USD VALUE: _____

CRYPTO
TRADING LOG BOOK

TRADING DETAILS

| ○ BUY ○ PROFIT | DATE TIME: | ENTRY PRICE: | PAIR: |
| ○ SELL ○ LOSS | DATE TIME: | EXIT PRICE: | |

MENTAL STATE

EXIT CONDITION

SETUP

NOTES

SATOSH W.L: _____ % OF ACCOUNT: _____ USD VALUE: _____

TRADING DETAILS

| ○ BUY ○ PROFIT | DATE TIME: | ENTRY PRICE: | PAIR: |
| ○ SELL ○ LOSS | DATE TIME: | EXIT PRICE: | |

MENTAL STATE

EXIT CONDITION

SETUP

NOTES

SATOSH W.L: _____ % OF ACCOUNT: _____ USD VALUE: _____

CRYPTO
TRADING LOG BOOK

TRADING DETAILS

| ○ BUY ○ PROFIT | DATE TIME: | ENTRY PRICE: | PAIR: |
| ○ SELL ○ LOSS | DATE TIME: | EXIT PRICE: | |

MENTAL STATE

EXIT CONDITION

SETUP

NOTES

SATOSH W.L: _____ % OF ACCOUNT: _____ USD VALUE: _____

TRADING DETAILS

| ○ BUY ○ PROFIT | DATE TIME: | ENTRY PRICE: | PAIR: |
| ○ SELL ○ LOSS | DATE TIME: | EXIT PRICE: | |

MENTAL STATE

EXIT CONDITION

SETUP

NOTES

SATOSH W.L: _____ % OF ACCOUNT: _____ USD VALUE: _____

CRYPTO
TRADING LOG BOOK

TRADING DETAILS

| ○ BUY ○ PROFIT | DATE TIME: | ENTRY PRICE: | PAIR: |
| ○ SELL ○ LOSS | DATE TIME: | EXIT PRICE: | |

MENTAL STATE

EXIT CONDITION

SETUP

NOTES

SATOSH W.L:_____ % OF ACCOUNT:_____ USD VALUE:_____

TRADING DETAILS

| ○ BUY ○ PROFIT | DATE TIME: | ENTRY PRICE: | PAIR: |
| ○ SELL ○ LOSS | DATE TIME: | EXIT PRICE: | |

MENTAL STATE

EXIT CONDITION

SETUP

NOTES

SATOSH W.L:_____ % OF ACCOUNT:_____ USD VALUE:_____

CRYPTO
TRADING LOG BOOK

TRADING DETAILS

| ○ BUY ○ PROFIT | DATE TIME: | ENTRY PRICE: | PAIR: |
| ○ SELL ○ LOSS | DATE TIME: | EXIT PRICE: | |

MENTRAL STATE

EXIT CONDITION

SETUP

NOTES

SATOSH W.L: _____ % OF ACCOUNT: _____ USD VALUE: _____

TRADING DETAILS

| ○ BUY ○ PROFIT | DATE TIME: | ENTRY PRICE: | PAIR: |
| ○ SELL ○ LOSS | DATE TIME: | EXIT PRICE: | |

MENTAL STATE

EXIT CONDITION

SETUP

NOTES

SATOSH W.L: _____ % OF ACCOUNT: _____ USD VALUE: _____

CRYPTO
TRADING LOG BOOK

TRADING DETAILS

| ○ BUY ○ PROFIT | DATE TIME: | ENTRY PRICE: | PAIR: |
| ○ SELL ○ LOSS | DATE TIME: | EXIT PRICE: | |

MENTAL STATE

EXIT CONDITION

SETUP

NOTES

SATOSH W.L: _____ % OF ACCOUNT: _____ USD VALUE: _____

TRADING DETAILS

| ○ BUY ○ PROFIT | DATE TIME: | ENTRY PRICE: | PAIR: |
| ○ SELL ○ LOSS | DATE TIME: | EXIT PRICE: | |

MENTAL STATE

EXIT CONDITION

SETUP

NOTES

SATOSH W.L: _____ % OF ACCOUNT: _____ USD VALUE: _____

CRYPTO
TRADING LOG BOOK

TRADING DETAILS

| ○ BUY ○ PROFIT | DATE TIME: | ENTRY PRICE: | PAIR: |
| ○ SELL ○ LOSS | DATE TIME: | EXIT PRICE: | |

MENTAL STATE

EXIT CONDITION

SETUP

NOTES

SATOSH W.L: _____ % OF ACCOUNT: _____ USD VALUE: _____

TRADING DETAILS

| ○ BUY ○ PROFIT | DATE TIME: | ENTRY PRICE: | PAIR: |
| ○ SELL ○ LOSS | DATE TIME: | EXIT PRICE: | |

MENTAL STATE

EXIT CONDITION

SETUP

NOTES

SATOSH W.L: _____ % OF ACCOUNT: _____ USD VALUE: _____

CRYPTO
TRADING LOG BOOK

TRADING DETAILS

| ○ BUY   ○ PROFIT | DATE TIME: | ENTRY PRICE: | PAIR: |
| ○ SELL ○ LOSS | DATE TIME: | EXIT PRICE: | |

MENTAL STATE | EXIT CONDITION

SETUP | NOTES

SATOSH W.L: _____ % OF ACCOUNT: _____ USD VALUE: _____

TRADING DETAILS

| ○ BUY   ○ PROFIT | DATE TIME: | ENTRY PRICE: | PAIR: |
| ○ SELL ○ LOSS | DATE TIME: | EXIT PRICE: | |

MENTAL STATE | EXIT CONDITION

SETUP | NOTES

SATOSH W.L: _____ % OF ACCOUNT: _____ USD VALUE: _____

CRYPTO
TRADING LOG BOOK

TRADING DETAILS

| ○ BUY ○ PROFIT | DATE TIME: | ENTRY PRICE: | PAIR: |
| ○ SELL ○ LOSS | DATE TIME: | EXIT PRICE: | |

MENTAL STATE

EXIT CONDITION

SETUP

NOTES

SATOSH W.L:_____ % OF ACCOUNT:_____ USD VALUE:_____

TRADING DETAILS

| ○ BUY ○ PROFIT | DATE TIME: | ENTRY PRICE: | PAIR: |
| ○ SELL ○ LOSS | DATE TIME: | EXIT PRICE: | |

MENTAL STATE

EXIT CONDITION

SETUP

NOTES

SATOSH W.L:_____ % OF ACCOUNT:_____ USD VALUE:_____

CRYPTO
TRADING LOG BOOK

TRADING DETAILS

| ○ BUY   ○ PROFIT | DATE TIME: | ENTRY PRICE: | PAIR: |
| ○ SELL ○ LOSS | DATE TIME: | EXIT PRICE: | |

MENTAL STATE

EXIT CONDITION

SETUP

NOTES

SATOSH W.L: _____ % OF ACCOUNT: _____ USD VALUE: _____

TRADING DETAILS

| ○ BUY   ○ PROFIT | DATE TIME: | ENTRY PRICE: | PAIR: |
| ○ SELL ○ LOSS | DATE TIME: | EXIT PRICE: | |

MENTAL STATE

EXIT CONDITION

SETUP

NOTES

SATOSH W.L: _____ % OF ACCOUNT: _____ USD VALUE: _____

CRYPTO
TRADING LOG BOOK

TRADING DETAILS

○ BUY ○ PROFIT	DATE TIME:	ENTRY PRICE:	PAIR:
○ SELL ○ LOSS	DATE TIME:	EXIT PRICE:	

MENTAL STATE

EXIT CONDITION

SETUP

NOTES

SATOSH W.L: _____ % OF ACCOUNT: _____ USD VALUE: _____

TRADING DETAILS

○ BUY ○ PROFIT	DATE TIME:	ENTRY PRICE:	PAIR:
○ SELL ○ LOSS	DATE TIME:	EXIT PRICE:	

MENTAL STATE

EXIT CONDITION

SETUP

NOTES

SATOSH W.L: _____ % OF ACCOUNT: _____ USD VALUE: _____